MENTAL HEALTH CRISIS

Teen Suicide

ON THE RISE

Bradley Steffens

ReferencePoint
Press

San Diego, CA

ReferencePoint Press®

About the Author

Bradley Steffens is a novelist, poet, and award-winning author of more than sixty nonfiction books for children and young adults. He is also a suicide survivor. His thirty-three-year-old son Ezekiel took his life in July 2014. This book is dedicated to his memory.

For more information, contact:
ReferencePoint Press, Inc.
PO Box 27779
San Diego, CA 92198
www.ReferencePointPress.com

Picture Credits:
Cover: BCFC/Shutterstock.com
 6: Daisy Daisy/Shutterstock.com
10: Mario Arango/iStock
12: shisu_ka/Shutterstock.com
15: tulpahn/Shutterstock.com
20: Maury Aaseng
23: Monkey Business Images/Shutterstock.com
27: Maksim Shmeljov/Shutterstock.com
31: William Perugini/Shutterstock.com
34: Kseniia Perminova/Shutterstock.com
39: fizkes/Shutterstock.com
41: Dan76/Shutterstock.com
45: New Africa/Shutterstock.com
49: fizkes/Shutterstock.com
52: Alexander Raths/Shutterstock.com
55: Tada Images/Shutterstock.com

LIBRARY OF CONGRESS CATALOGING-IN-PUBLICATION DATA

Names: Steffens, Bradley, 1955- author.
Title: Teen suicide on the rise / Bradley Steffens.
Description: San Diego, CA : ReferencePoint Press, [2022] | Series: Mental health crisis | Includes bibliographical references and index.
Identifiers: LCCN 2021059092 (print) | LCCN 2021059093 (ebook) | ISBN 9781678202804 (library binding) | ISBN 9781678202811 (ebook)
Subjects: LCSH: Teenagers--Suicidal behavior--Juvenile literature.
Classification: LCC HV6546 .S73 2022 (print) | LCC HV6546 (ebook) | DDC 362.280835--dc23/eng/20220203
LC record available at https://lccn.loc.gov/2021059092
LC ebook record available at https://lccn.loc.gov/2021059093

CONTENTS

A Troubling Trend

Three days before his thirteenth birthday in April 2020, Hayden Hunstable was playing his favorite video game, *Fortnite*, in his bedroom. For weeks during the COVID-19 pandemic, playing video games with his buddies was the only social contact Hayden had. His school had closed, and, like millions of other students, Hayden was participating in remote learning via online video.

Impulsive Actions

A few months earlier, Hayden's parents had purchased a large, high-quality computer monitor for Hayden's gaming enjoyment. One day, in February 2020, Hayden made a mistake while playing *Fortnite*, causing his team to lose. A top gamer for his age and extremely competitive, Hayden was deeply upset by his play. As he left his bedroom, he threw his gaming controller over his shoulder in disgust. It crashed into the center of the new monitor and broke it.

When Hayden told his parents what he had done, his father, Brad, said that he did not care about the broken monitor, but he did care about how Hayden had acted. Hayden's parents said he could earn a new monitor by doing chores around the house and being nice to his younger sister. Hayden responded well, and his parents bought a new monitor for him. It was not as nice as the one he had broken, but it was serviceable. On April 17, 2020, Hayden accidentally broke that monitor as well. Anxious because of the school closings, angry at himself for breaking the monitor, and ashamed that he had disappointed his parents again, Hayden went into his closet and hung himself. His eight-year-old sister found him a few minutes later and alerted their father. Brad Hunstable frantically tried to revive his son, using cardiac pulmonary resuscitation and an automatic electronic defibrillator that he had in the house in case of an emergency. Nothing worked. Hayden had taken his own life.

"He's gone," says Hunstable. "It's permanent. It's freakin' permanent. And you don't even know what to think or how to feel. You're mad. You're angry. You're shocked. You're sad. You're questioning everything. You're mad at yourself. The guilt. You let him down."[1]

The Effects of School Closings

Hunstable believes the school closures during the pandemic contributed to his son's suicide. "Social isolation is hard enough for adults. It's even harder for our kids,"[2] he says. "Covid killed my son, but not in the way you might think, and I do believe that. We were seeing increased anxiety from the pandemic and that was clear. He wanted to play football, he wanted to see his friends. You know, he couldn't have a birthday, it was four days away. He hated online schooling, some kids love it, my son hated it."[3]

Hunstable's beliefs about the effects of the pandemic on his son have been borne out by research conducted by the Centers for Disease Control and Prevention (CDC), an agency of the federal government. The CDC found that emergency department visits for suspected suicide attempts among twelve- to seventeen-year-olds skyrocketed during the pandemic. Suspected suicide attempts among adolescents rose 22 percent during summer 2020 compared

> "Covid killed my son, but not in the way you might think, and I do believe that. We were seeing increased anxiety from the pandemic and that was clear."[3]
>
> —Brad Hunstable, whose son, Hayden, took his life at age twelve

to summer 2019. By winter 2021, the number of suspected suicide attempts was 39 percent higher than it was in winter 2019.

By December 2021, the situation was so dire that US Surgeon General Vivek Murthy issued a formal advisory, warning health care professionals and the public that America's youth were in the grips of a mental health crisis. The crisis had been building for years, Murthy said, but the pandemic had made it worse. "The pandemic era's unfathomable number of deaths, pervasive sense of fear, economic instability, and forced physical distancing from loved ones, friends, and communities have exacerbated the unprecedented stresses young people already faced," Murthy declared. "Mental health challenges in children, adolescents, and young adults are real, and they are widespread."[4]

According to preliminary 2020 data gathered by the CDC, the suicide rate among adolescents did not rise during the pandemic, but it did not decline either. This reversed a hopeful trend that had started in 2019, in which the annual suicide rate per one hundred thousand adolescents had declined for the first time in twenty years.

According to the US Surgeon General, America's youth are in the grips of a mental health crisis.

It seems that the pandemic stopped that progress in its tracks.

Even with the short-lived decline, the suicide rate for ten- to nineteen-year-olds more than doubled from 2007 to 2019, according to the National Center for Health Statistics. Even worse, it quadrupled for ten- to fourteen-year-olds during that period. Suicide remains the second-leading cause of adolescent death, behind only accidental deaths.

A Suicide Survivor's Hopes

Brad Hunstable hopes that his son's story will serve as a wake-up call to parents, teachers, and friends of young people who might be suffering during the pandemic. In an open to letter to his late son, Hunstable encourages families to talk about suicide:

> Dear Hayden,
>
> We're sorry we let you down. You didn't deserve this. We should have been there for you. This wasn't your fault. We didn't know how to have that conversation with you. We didn't know we needed to. We didn't know you weren't safe in your own room. . . .
>
> Suicide is still the second leading cause of death for eleven- to seventeen-year-olds. And we're not talking about it. So we should all start now. . . .
>
> Grandparents and parents, start the conversation. Don't let suicide finish it. Talk to your kids. Ask your kids if they've experienced disappointments and hurts. If they feel depressed. If they've ever thought of taking their life. If they say yes to any of these, take it seriously and create a plan together, should they ever feel like harming themselves.
>
> Let's stop reading statistics. And start preventing them. Conversations matter. Kids, talk more. Parents, listen. No one should be almost thirteen. Every Hayden deserves to see tomorrow. We can do better. Will do better.[5]

CHAPTER ONE

Social Media as a Risk Factor for Teen Girls

Anastasia Vlasova, an eighteen-year-old student who lives in Reston, Virginia, was thirteen when she opened her Instagram account. "I was super excited and I couldn't wait to post photos with all of those intense Instagram filters that no one really uses nowadays," Vlasova remembers. Like most users, Vlasova followed her friends, liking and commenting on their photos. She soon noticed the accounts of fitness influencers—individuals who post photos and videos about their healthy diets, recipes, and workouts. Vlasova found she was "incredible [sic] inspired" by them. "The fitness influencers that I follow were all super tan and very toned and a lot of them are smiling in their photos and they just looked like they were living basically the best life possible," she says. They became her heroes, and she wanted to be like them. "As a 13, 14, whatever year-old, looking at a 20-year-old who is super fit, super beautiful, has a bunch of followers, I really aspired be like them because they portrayed this image of perfection and of happiness."[6]

A Growing Obsession

Still just thirteen, Vlasova launched her own fitness account, posting recipes, motivational tips, and videos of herself playing tennis and working out. She gained such a large following that a sportswear company sent her free clothing to wear in her videos. The attention made her feel good. But secretly, she harbored doubts about her appearance. "I would go onto social media and I would use that as motivation, again, to get me to get back into fitness or go to the gym or eat healthy," she remembers. "But then as I closed the app, I would feel so awful about myself and I would look in the mirror and I would think, 'Oh my gosh, I am nowhere close to the image of these fitness influencers. I need to work out.'"[7]

> "As I closed the app, I would feel so awful about myself and I would look in the mirror and I would think, 'Oh my gosh, I am nowhere close to the image of these fitness influencers. I need to work out.'"[7]
>
> —Anastasia Vlasova, teen Instagram user

Vlasova became obsessed with her diet, showing signs of orthorexia, an unhealthy focus on eating in a healthy way. "At first I just started making healthier swaps with the food that I was consuming at the time," Vlasova recalls. "So instead of chips I had healthier whole grain crackers, and then it translated into a much more unhealthy relationship because I started to punish myself whenever I ate something that was considered an unhealthy food or fast food." One night, Vlasova ate a small dessert. She was so concerned about its effects that she had her mother take her to the gym late at night "just so I could run six miles and burn off what I had just consumed." Vlasova knew that the pressures she put on herself were harmful, but she could not resist. "I just accepted it that I was just going to live as this anxious human being with an eating disorder because of social media," she says. "And I did feel a little bit hopeless because I was like, 'Dang, I really don't want to continue my life living in so much pain and suffering and self-comparison and a little bit of depression and anxiety and eating disorder, but I also don't want to give Instagram up.'"[8]

As Vlasova's presence on social media grew, her mental health continued to deteriorate. One day, when she was in eleventh grade, Vlasova met with her school counselor. "I said, 'I'm

Some social media influencers initially like the feedback they receive from their fans. Once the excitement of new followers and positive comments wears off, they feel extra pressure to maintain their perfect image.

having suicidal thoughts,'" Vlasova recalls. "I told her I don't want to be here anymore, I hate myself. I hate how much I have disconnected from my friends and just from who I truly am because of the stupid eating disorder and my depression and my anxiety, and I don't know what to do."[9]

Documented Harm

Vlasova is not the only young woman who traces her mental health struggles to her involvement with Instagram. Internal research conducted by Facebook, which owns Instagram, found that 21 percent of female teen users say that Instagram makes them feel worse about themselves. The negative effects are even greater for teens who are concerned with their body image, as Vlasova was. The researchers reported that 32 percent of teen girls with Instagram accounts said that when they felt bad about their bodies, Instagram made them feel worse. "We make body image issues worse for one in three teen girls,"[10] stated a slide in a presentation the researchers prepared for company management.

10

Most teens surveyed in the Facebook studies did not report negative feelings related to using Instagram. The majority had positive feeling about the app. They enjoyed using it to express themselves, to connect with friends, and to form new online relationships. But a significant percentage of Instagram users report having negative feelings after using Instagram. The greatest concentration of negative feelings is among teen girls. When asked if any of the things they have felt in the last month started on Instagram, a significant percentage of teen girls said yes. They listed several negative feelings, including,

Not attractive—41 percent

Have to create the perfect image—39 percent

Don't have enough friends—32 percent

Not good enough—24 percent

Friends aren't really their friends—24 percent

Alone or lonely—21 percent

Down, sad, or depressed—10 percent[11]

Making Things Worse

Instagram poses special risks for teens who are already struggling with their mental health. The Facebook researchers found that 31 percent of teens with mental health issues said that Instagram made their mental health worse. "Young people are acutely aware that Instagram can be bad for their mental health, yet feel compelled to spend time on the app for fear of missing out on cultural and social trends,"[12] states one of the Facebook research slides.

Some teens get trapped in a downward spiral of feeling bad, checking Instagram to feel better, and, instead, feeling worse. "Teens blame Instagram for increases in the rate of anxiety and depression,"[13] the Facebook researchers stated on another slide. In a crucial finding, the researchers reported that the teens brought up the connection to Instagram without being asked about it. Most alarmingly, among teens who reported wanting to hurt themselves, 9 percent said their feelings started on Instagram, and among those having suicidal thoughts, 6 percent linked their desire to take their own lives to their use of the photo-sharing app.

Designed for Comparison

One of the most toxic aspects of Instagram is the way it allows and even encourages teens—especially girls—to compare themselves to other users, including celebrities, models, and fitness influencers. The comparisons to photos of glamorous and super-fit users often make the teens feel worse about themselves. "Comparisons on Instagram can change how young women view and describe themselves,"[14] states the Facebook internal research. "I've had to stop myself looking at Instagram in the morning because it has so much power to shape how I feel,"[15] one female user told the Facebook researchers.

A significant percentage of Instagram users say they experience negative feelings after using the app. The biggest concentration of users experiencing those feelings is among teen girls.

Whistleblower Calls for Facebook CEO to Resign

In September 2021, Facebook's internal research revealing the dangers that Instagram poses to teen girls was leaked to the public by former Facebook employee Frances Haugen. The research documents that Haugen smuggled out of the social media giant show that Facebook and Instagram executives were fully aware of the dangers posed by their social media platforms. Based on those findings, Haugen called for Facebook CEO Mark Zuckerberg to resign. "I think Facebook would be stronger with someone who was willing to focus on safety," Haugen told journalist Laurie Segall in November 2021. "I find it unconscionable that, as you read through the documents, it states very clearly there needs to be more resources on very basic safety systems," Haugen said. "And instead of investing on making sure that our platforms are a minimal level of safe, they're about to invest ten thousand engineers in video games and I can't imagine how this makes sense."

Quoted in Lauren Feiner, "Facebook Whistleblower Haugen Says Zuckerberg Should Step Down as CEO," CNBC, November 1, 2021. www.cnbc.com.

These comparisons are not always made by teens who are searching out pictures by themselves. Instead, an Instagram feature known as "Explore" automatically serves up a never-ending stream of photos of toned and beautiful models to any user who has liked such images in the past. Immersion in these images can be harmful to some users.

Iris Tsouris, an eighteen-year-old freshman at Yale University is one of those who was swept up in Instagram's flood of images and tips that suggest a better life awaits. Her Explore page showed her countless lifestyle and body images that played on her insecurities. Some posts even suggested that she replace some of her meals with iced coffee to reduce her calorie intake. "It perpetuates negative self-image in people, stuff that might feed into eating disorders," says Tsouris. "I've definitely seen people impacted by jealousy or the fear of missing out."[16]

A former Instagram executive suggests that comparisons are not merely a by-product of using the app; they are part of the software design. "People use Instagram because it's a competition," says the executive. "That's the fun part."[17]

Facebook's research suggests that Instagram is more harmful than its rivals, including Snapchat and TikTok. "Social comparison is worse on Instagram,"[18] said Facebook researchers who examined teen attitudes toward the various photo-sharing apps. The differences lie within the programming of the apps. Instagram's Explore focuses on the body, but Snapchat's abundance of funny filters emphasizes the face. TikTok promotes the videos that are most popular overall rather than ones appealing to the specific interests of a particular user. The mix of videos keeps TikTok users from dwelling on a certain kind of content, such as fitness and diet.

Academics were not surprised by the findings of the Facebook researchers. Jean Twenge, a psychology professor at San Diego State University and the lead author of several studies looking into the effects of social media on teens, says that the Facebook research only confirms what she has been documenting for years. "We've known from academic research for many years that the longer a teen girl spends on social media, the more likely she is to be depressed and to engage in behaviors like self-harm say like cutting," says Twenge. "And we've known that the suicide rate has doubled for ten- to-fourteen-year-olds since 2007, and it's quadrupled for girls in that age group right as social media became popular [from 1999 to 2018]."[19]

> "The longer a teen girl spends on social media, the more likely she is to be depressed and to engage in behaviors like self-harm say like cutting."[19]
>
> —Jean Twenge, professor of psychology at San Diego State University

Keeping a Corporate Secret

In March 2021, Congress called Facebook's chief executive officer (CEO), Mark Zuckerberg, to testify about claims that Face-

Researchers employed by Instagram's owner, Facebook, say that one of the most toxic aspects of Instagram is the way it allows and even encourages teens to compare themselves to celebrities, models, and fitness influencers.

book was one of several online platforms that contributed to the spread of misinformation. In the session, Representative Cathy McMorris Rodgers of Washington directly asked him if consuming social media content is harmful to children's mental health. "I don't think that the research is conclusive on that," Zuckerberg replied. "But I can summarize what I have learned, if that is helpful. . . . Overall, the research that we have seen is that using social apps to connect with other people can have positive mental health benefits and well-being benefits by helping people feel more connected and less lonely."[20]

In August 2021, Senators Richard Blumenthal of Connecticut and Marsha Blackburn of Tennessee wrote a letter to Zuckerberg, asking if Facebook had any evidence that it might have harmful effects on teens. The company wrote back, "We are not aware. We are not aware of a consensus among studies or experts about how much screen time is too much."[21] When Facebook's internal research revealing the harms to teen girls became public, Blumenthal was outraged, stating that the response he and Blackburn had received from Facebook "was simply untrue." Blumenthal continued,

Facebook knows. It knows the evidence of harm to teens is substantial and specific to Instagram. . . . Its own comprehensive internal review indicated that Facebook employees found, and I quote, "Substantial evidence suggests that experiences on Instagram and Facebook make body dissatisfaction worse, particularly viewing attractive images of others, viewing filtered images, posting selfies, and viewing content with certain [hashtags]." . . . Facebook knows the destructive consequences that Instagram's design and algorithms are having on our young people in our society, but it has routinely prioritized its own rapid growth over basic safety for our children.[22]

Searching for Answers

Adam Mosseri, the head of Instagram, has been more forthcoming about the potential dangers posed by the photo-sharing platform, but he disputes the idea that such harms originate on social media. "Social comparison, anxiety, these problems aren't Instagram-specific problems, they're societal problems," Mosseri told Georgia Wells of the *Wall Street Journal*. Nevertheless, Mosseri admits social media can make the situation worse. "I think there's way more upside than there is downside but I do think there are downsides and we need to embrace that reality and do everything we can to address them as effectively as we can."[23]

Instagram has looked into ways to help improve the mental health of teen users. For example, researchers learned that many teens linked how they felt about themselves to the number of likes they received for photos they shared. To help users avoid rating

> "Facebook knows the destructive consequences that Instagram's design and algorithms are having on our young people in our society, but it has routinely prioritized its own rapid growth over basic safety for our children."[22]
>
> —Richard Blumenthal, US senator from Connecticut

themselves, the company created a feature that enabled users to hide the number of likes they received. In an experiment known as Project Daisy that began in 2019, Instagram made the feature available to a limited number of users. After monitoring the project for more than a year, researchers concluded that hiding likes did not seem to affect the well-being of users, neither improving nor harming their mental health. In May 2021, the company made the feature available to all users, believing the company would benefit from the appearance of trying to make things better for its users.

Instagram has also experimented with a feature that encourages users to take a break from the app after a certain period. Another experimental feature is designed to steer users toward positive, uplifting content. For now, however, the best solution for teens being harmed by the app might be to do what Anastasia Vlasova did: delete it. "I really don't want to go back," Vlasova says. "The pros no longer outweigh the cons of using social media and I feel so awesome. And so I guess what I did after it was finally start living my life. I'm more laid back I feel than when I had Instagram."[24]

The Impact of the Pandemic on Teen Mental Health

Before the COVID-19 pandemic struck the United States, Rodney Moore Jr. was a fun-loving fourteen-year-old student in Anaheim, California. He loved animals, played saxophone, and was a good student who enjoyed school. Not surprisingly, Rodney was disappointed when his school district canceled in-person schooling. Online learning was not for him. He missed his friends, he began to lose interest in his schoolwork, and his grades suffered. Worst of all, he began to have doubts about his future. "He kept on saying, 'I don't see the point. Nothing's going to get better,' is what he would say,"[25] remembers his mother, Adriana Moore.

Isolated and hopeless, Rodney took his own life. "We felt that something was going the other direction, but we never knew to this degree," says his father, Rodney Moore Sr. "Although the coronavirus didn't take my son's life directly, it took it indirectly is how I feel."[26]

A Pandemic Within a Pandemic

Each suicide is the result of a unique combination of risk factors, including biological and environmental ones, but it appears that the measures taken by authorities to cope with the COVID-19 pandemic have hit teenagers especially hard. School closures, homeschooling, and mask wearing have all affected teens' lifestyles and, in many cases, their mental health. Heather Huszti, the chief psychologist at Children's Hospital of Orange County—the county Rodney Moore Jr. called home—told NBC News in January 2021 that the number of calls she had received from parents concerned about their children's mental health had doubled from the year before, when the coronavirus had yet to be confirmed in the United States.

> "We are seeing our pediatric emergency departments and our inpatient units overrun with kids attempting suicide and suffering from other forms of major mental health illness."[27]
>
> —Jena Hausmann, the CEO of Children's Hospital Colorado

The same trend was apparent across the country. In May 2021, CEO Jena Hausmann of Children's Hospital Colorado in Aurora, Colorado, declared a state of emergency in pediatric mental health—the first in the hospital's 117-year history. "We are seeing our pediatric emergency departments and our inpatient units overrun with kids attempting suicide and suffering from other forms of major mental health illness,"[27] said Hausmann. "I've been in practice for over 20 years in pediatrics, and I've never seen anything like the demand for mental health services we've seen at Children's [Hospital] Colorado in the past 15 months," said David Brumbaugh, the hospital's chief medical officer. "There have been many weeks in 2021 that the No. 1 reason for presenting to our emergency department is a suicide attempt. Our kids have run out of resilience—their tanks are empty."[28]

Concerned about the reports of deteriorating mental health across the nation, the CDC conducted a survey of 5,412 adults during the week of June 24 through June 30, 2020. The researchers found that 75 percent of young adults, which includes eighteen- and nineteen-year-olds, reported struggling with at least one adverse mental or behavioral health condition related to the COVID-19 pandemic. Almost two-thirds—63 percent—reported having symptoms

Declining Teen Mental Health

In December 2021 the US Surgeon General issued a rare warning: America's youth were experiencing a mental health crisis before the pandemic—and that crisis has worsened as a result of the pandemic. The steady decline in teen mental health is evident in the most recent National Youth Risk Behavior Survey. That survey, conducted every other year by the Centers for Disease Control and Prevention, covers 2009 to 2019. It finds that feelings of sadness and hopelessness have been steadily rising among American teenagers—and with those feelings have come an increase in thoughts about suicide, suicide planning, and suicide attempts.

The percentage of high school students who:	2009 Total	2011 Total	2013 Total	2015 Total	2017 Total	2019 Total
Experienced persistent feelings of sadness or hopelessness	26.1%	28.5%	29.9%	29.9%	31.5%	36.7%
Seriously considered attempting suicide	13.8%	15.8%	17.0%	17.7%	17.2%	18.8%
Made a suicide plan	10.9%	12.8%	13.6%	14.6%	13.6%	15.7%
Attempted suicide	6.3%	7.8%	8.0%	8.6%	7.4%	8.9%
Were injured in a suicide attempt that had to be treated by a doctor or nurse	1.9%	2.4%	2.7%	2.8%	2.4%	2.5%

Source: National Youth Risk Behavior Surveys, 2009–2019, Centers for Disease Control and Prevention. www.cdc.gov/healthyyouth/data/yrbs/pdf/YRBSDataSummaryTrendsReport2019-508.pdf.

of anxiety or depression. Even worse, 25 percent of eighteen- to twenty-four-year-olds reported having seriously considered taking their own lives in the past thirty days. This did not mean that the thought of suicide had merely flashed through their minds. Rather, they had prolonged thoughts about taking their own lives. These prolonged thoughts about suicide are known as suicidal ideation, and they often are a prelude to suicide attempts and suicide deaths.

Risks for Teen Girls

As reports of suicidal ideation and attempts flooded into the CDC, the agency launched another mental health study in 2021, using data from the National Syndromic Surveillance Program, which gathers health information from state and local hospitals. The CDC studied the records from 71 percent of the nation's emergency departments in forty-nine states and the District of Columbia. The researchers looked at emergency department visits among male and female patients aged twelve to twenty-five for three periods between January 1, 2019—before the pandemic—and May 15, 2021. The results were shocking.

Beginning in May 2020, following school closures in forty-eight states, emergency department visits for suspected suicide attempts began increasing among twelve- to seventeen-year-olds, especially among girls. During the survey period, which ended in August 2020, the average weekly number of emergency department visits for suspected suicide attempts among teenage girls was 26 percent higher than for the same period in 2019. By March 2021, that number had soared to more than 50 percent higher than for the same period in 2019. "The findings from this study suggest more severe distress among young females than has been identified in previous reports during the pandemic, reinforcing the need for increased attention to, and prevention for, this population,"[29] wrote the researchers. The study is "a very significant signal to pay attention to young people and especially adolescent girls," says Christine Yu Moutier, the chief medical officer at the American Foundation for Suicide Prevention. "This is really, in a way, a ring-the-alarm moment that distress is mounting so much that it's overwhelming coping strategies."[30]

The number of emergency department visits for suspected suicide attempts also rose among teen boys. From February to March 2021, that rate rose 3.7 percent among boys compared to the same period in 2019. Even though the number is lower for boys, it is still troubling because a higher rate of boys complete their suicides than do girls. This is because boys tend to use more lethal methods than girls do. According to the CDC, discharging a firearm is the most common method of suicide among males, whereas poisoning is the most common method of suicide for females.

Why Is Mental Health Worsening in the United States?

Journalist Glenn Greenwald is an observer of American culture. In this excerpt from an article on The Intercept website, Greenwald explores the effect of the pandemic on mental health:

> In a remotely healthy society, one that provides basic emotional needs to its population, suicide and serious suicidal ideation are rare events. It is anathema to the most basic human instinct: the will to live. A society in which such a vast swath of the population is seriously considering it as an option is one which is anything but healthy, one which is plainly failing to provide its citizens the basic necessities for a fulfilling life. . . .
>
> What makes these trends all the more disturbing is that they long predated the arrival of the coronavirus crisis. . . .
>
> One answer was provided by Dr. Laurel Williams, chief of psychiatry at Texas Children's Hospital, to NBC when discussing the rise of depression: "There's a lack of community. There's the amount of time that we spend in front of screens and not in front of other people. If you don't have a community to reach out to, then your hopelessness doesn't have any place to go."

Glenn Greenwald, "The Social Fabric of the U.S. Is Fraying Severely, If Not Unravelling," The Intercept, August 28, 2020. https://theintercept.com.

Not only have the number of emergency department visits for adolescent suicide attempts risen at some hospitals, but so have the number of hospital admissions for adolescents who are suicidal. "The kids that we are seeing now in the emergency department are really at the stage of maybe even having tried or attempted or have a detailed plan," says Vera Feuer, the director of pediatric emergency psychiatry at Cohen Children's Medical Center of Northwell Health in New York. "And we're admitting to the hospital more kids than usual because of how unwell they are."[31]

Reversing a Promising Trend

The CDC researchers emphasized that the number of suicide attempts did not necessarily mean that the number of suicide deaths had increased among teens in 2020 and 2021. However, it did appear that the small decline in suicide deaths in that age group that had begun in 2019 had come to an end. Complete data for 2020 suicides was not yet available. However, provisional data showed that although the suicide rate for older adults decreased in the period of July through September 2020 compared to the same period the year before, "the suicide rate among young persons aged 15–24 years during this same period saw no significant change." This is concerning because suicide rates had declined

Although suicide attempts are less common among boys than among girls, the statistics are alarming because boys succeed in suicide attempts at a higher rate than girls do.

A Fourteen-Year-Old Loses Hope

When she was fourteen, Lily Allen decided to end her life. Now twenty, she looks back at that fateful night:

> I was deep in my depression hole, crying in my room. I honestly felt like the world was ending, all the walls were closing in on me. I couldn't breathe. I was like, there's no way to get better. . . .
>
> The rational part of me was like, it gets better than high school, but then the very emotional, sad, beaten-down child part of me was like, there is no way out of this. I think it was my last ditch-effort to get help from a person who I could confide in more comfortably than my parents because I didn't even know how my parents were going to react when I told them I was depressed. It wasn't a thing we talked about in our house.

Allen texted a suicide note to a friend, and the friend contacted the police. The officers told Allen's parents, and they took her to a hospital, where she stayed for eight days. Allen says that she was "super depressed" during the pandemic, but she used the skills she learned in the hospital to survive.

Quoted in Maura Hohman, "Girls Are Attempting Suicide More During the Pandemic. Here's How Parents Can Help," *Today*, September 29, 2021. www.today.com.

among young adults aged fifteen to twenty-four, decreasing from 14.49 per 100,000 in 2018 to 13.95 per 100,000 in 2019. It was the first time the young adult suicide death rate had declined in more than twenty years. The CDC report suggests that the pandemic stopped the decline of suicide deaths in this age group.

"These increases (in suicidal ideation and behavior) were apparent even before the COVID pandemic, but have worsened over the time of this pandemic," says Beth Kennard, the director of the Suicide Prevention and Resilience program at Children's Health in Dallas, Texas. "We believe that's partially because of higher levels of social isolation . . . more difficulty in school with the online format, and economic pressure and stress on the family, which translates to the kid."[32]

A Loss of Hope

Anthony Orr, a high school senior in Las Vegas, was one of those who suffered from the pressures and isolation of the pandemic. Orr was getting close to high school graduation when the school district closed in March 2020. "He was looking forward to all of the senior activities, prom and graduation," remembers his mother, Pamela Orr. But the COVID pandemic altered his plans. Prom was canceled, and instead of a traditional graduation, Orr and a few other students—all wearing surgical masks along with their caps and gowns—participated in a smaller, socially distanced ceremony. "That was the most we could do because of COVID,"[33] says his mother.

> "These increases (in suicidal ideation and behavior) were apparent even before the COVID pandemic, but have worsened over the time of this pandemic."[32]
>
> —Beth Kennard, the director of suicide prevention at Children's Health in Dallas, Texas

An honors student, Orr postponed going to college. "Right now . . . it's all online, and you just lose the whole college experience," explained Pamela Orr, recalling her son's decision to wait until in-person classes resumed. He took a job in the construction industry, and all appeared well on the surface. "He seemed happy to us," remembers his mother. "He seemed happy."[34] Inside, however, Orr was losing hope that his life would ever live up to his dreams. In August 2020, Anthony Orr took his own life.

A Lack of Warning Signs

Orr's parents were shocked. Their son had no history of mental illness or suicidal ideation. It used to be thought that 90 percent of suicides were related to mental illness, but research published by the CDC in June 2018 found that the actual number of suicides with a diagnosed mental illness was just 46 percent. The other 54 percent of suicides were people, like Orr, who did not have a mental health condition but were struggling with various life stressors.

Suicides with no previous signs are even more prevalent among teens, whose brains are still developing and, as a result, are not as well equipped as adults to handle difficulties. "With this population, it's the perfect storm for life to be extra difficult," says Lauren Anderson, the executive director of the Josh Anderson Foundation in Vienna, Virginia, a nonprofit suicide prevention organization. "Based on the development of the brain, they are more inclined to risky behavior, to decide in that moment."[35]

Orr's parents struggled to cope with the loss of their son. "Sleep is elusive," says Pamela Orr. "Any time can be a hard time. I mean, I can be in the grocery store, and I see his favorite breakfast cereal, and I just have to stop what I'm doing and just leave because anything, everything can be a trigger for the intense sadness."[36]

Orr's father, Marc, feels that the health care system failed Anthony. "They get well-checks, you know," he says. "Insurance pays for a well-check. But there's not any mental [health] screening that's done or emotional screening."[37]

Those Most at Risk

Hayden Hunstable, Rodney Moore, Anthony Orr, and a large percentage of adolescents who have taken their lives had no prior mental health diagnoses. But the teens who were most at risk during the pandemic were those with underlying mental health conditions, including anxiety, depression, and substance abuse. "They have difficulties with their mood or difficulties with learning or socialization or medical issues," says Feuer. "And now you have other layers of difficulties on top of that. These are the kids we see in real hopeless moments."[38]

One of the problems for at-risk teens is that the pandemic disrupted the in-person care they may have been receiving from a therapist or school counselor. According to Dr. Susan Duffy, a professor of pediatrics and emergency medicine at Brown University, many troubled teens were in relatively stable condition thanks to the outpatient care they were receiving. But the pandemic changed all that. Duffy herself treated a thirteen-year-old girl who had come to her hospital's emergency department after a suicide attempt. The teen had been receiving at-home and in-school care for her anxiety and depression. When those services were suspended, the teen's mental health deteriorated. She fell behind in her schoolwork, engaged in self-harm, and eventually tried to take her own life. "It was her [older] teenage sister who found her in the bathroom and who called their mother, who had to leave work,"[39] Duffy recalls.

Experts say that the social isolation caused by the COVID-19 pandemic made the problem of teen depression and suicide worse.

Remote learning has also made it harder for teachers and counselors to pick up on signs that a student is struggling emotionally. Colleen Neely, a counselor at Shadow Ridge High School near Las Vegas, told NPR about the difficulties of adequately caring for students during the school closures. One of her students had emotional issues relating to his family life. At one point he had been homeless, and the school had helped him find a local family that took him in. "He was a smart, shy kind of kid," Neely remembers. "Very kind, polite and respectful." Before the pandemic, Neely saw him daily. That ended in March 2020, when the school shut down and switched to online learning because of COVID-19. Neely kept in touch with her students via email, but it was not the same. "There are just extra barriers," Neely observes. "We're not there just in passing, or they can't go to their teacher and be like, 'Hey, I want to see my counselor.' They can't stop in at lunch. They have to make that effort with an email or clicking on a computer to make an appointment." In May 2020, just two weeks before graduation, the troubled teen took his own life. "I'd just sent him an email, telling him how proud I was of him," Neely recalls. "And that he was almost there. And the next phase of his life was going to start." Neely is haunted by the idea that the teen might still be alive were it not for the school closures. "Part of me will always question, if we had been in the building—and if he had been able to just see another adult, his friends, possibly talk to me—if things would have been different."[40]

The pandemic seems to have had several very different effects on teen suicide. On the one hand, the school closures and the workplace closures meant that suicidal teens were not alone as much as they would be under normal circumstances, as their parents were home with them. This likely prevented some suicides. On the other hand, the separation from friends, teachers, and counselors also robbed some students of the support systems they needed to keep their lives in balance. The loss of traditional support systems appears to have contributed to the rise in suicide attempts and may have caused some teens to take their own lives.

CHAPTER THREE

LGBTQ Teens at Risk

American society has come a long way in recognizing and embracing differences in genders and sexual preferences, but teens in the LGBTQ (lesbian, gay, bisexual, transgender, queer or questioning) community still face more teasing, bullying, and exclusion than other teens do. This victimization causes confusion, loneliness, and depression—all of which are risk factors for suicide.

Transgender individuals—those whose gender identity does not align with their biological sex—are especially at risk. A 2019 study by the CDC found that more than one-third of transgender youths (34.6 percent) reported having attempted suicide in the previous twelve months—a rate more than five times higher than that of their cisgender counterparts (those whose gender identity aligns with their biological sex).

Suicidal thoughts among transgender youths often grow out of the negative experiences they have because of their sexual identity. "Many young trans people experience discrimination, intolerance, bullying, rejection and violence from several spheres," says Juliet Jacques, a journalist who documented her gender transition in a blog.

First at school, a place where gender norms are enforced and policed, where you're told by teachers and other pupils that boys do x and girls do y. Within the family there can be rejection, verbal and physical abuse, and then also at [the] street level, in the media and in the workplace. Together this can render people unable to see a future for themselves. It is no wonder suicidal thoughts are so common.[41]

Shear Avory, who identifies as transgender, experienced isolation, intimidation, and violence in high school. "I was constantly in a space of being unaccepted, unwelcomed and put down," says Avory, who uses the personal identity pronouns *they/them/theirs*. Avory was beaten in the halls, spat on, and had their hair pulled. One day, someone scrawled "Get out faggot or die" on Avory's locker. "That's when I started really thinking about suicide," Avory says. "I just felt like: What's the point anymore? There's just no happiness. I don't see an end game. I don't see this getting any better."[42]

Avory faced the bullying as well as they could, but at times it was just too much. "I had been hospitalized after several breakdowns. I mean, breakdowns that would last for hours. I was screaming and panicking and crying and shaking, and I think at that time I had just had enough," remembers Avory. Under mental health care, Avory was diagnosed with anxiety and depression. "I didn't know what life was for me anymore. I really questioned my own self-worth and if I was going to be able to make it, and if I meant something to myself or anyone else."[43]

While still a teen, Avory moved into a queer collective in South Los Angeles. It was a place where Avory felt safe to explore their identity. "I was just myself then," Avory remembers. Avory's suicidal thoughts did not disappear al-

> "I was constantly in a space of being unaccepted, unwelcomed and put down. . . . That's when I started really thinking about suicide. . . . I just felt like: What's the point anymore? There's just no happiness. I don't see an end game. I don't see this getting any better."[42]
>
> —Shear Avory, a transgender person who has battled suicidal thoughts for years

together, but they were not as frequent. "Healing is not a linear experience," Avory says. "For so long I've been stuck in just wanting everything to disappear, from wanting the trauma to go away, for it to fade away from me, not to feel these feelings anymore." Eventually, Avory moved to Washington, DC, and began to see a therapist. The counseling is paying off. "I'm not going anywhere," Avory says. "I can take pride in knowing that I've already made something of myself. . . . I'm alive."[44]

Risks for Biological Females

Although all transgender teens have higher rates of suicide attempts than cisgender teens, researchers at the University of Arizona report that suicide risks are higher for some transgender groups than others.

In their 2018 study of 120,617 adolescents aged eleven to nineteen, the University of Arizona researchers found that 14 percent of all adolescents reported having attempted suicide at some point in their lives. Female adolescents reported more suicide attempts than male adolescents—17.6 percent for females and 9.8 percent for males. Similarly, within the transgender community, females transitioning to males reported a higher attempted suicide

Members of the LGBTQ community often face discrimination, isolation, bullying, and even violence in many areas, including school and work. To cope, LGBTQ individuals often turn to counseling, especially when they are feeling suicidal. Sadly, discrimination sometimes extends even into the world of therapy. An anonymous respondent to a survey conducted by the National LGBTQ Institute on Intimate Partner Violence reported a chilling experience:

> I wanted help getting away from my abusive partner, but the therapist made things worse and suggested that the abuse was my fault. I was suicidal, and the therapist did not take me seriously and did not provide emergency help. I suspect that my queerness and masculine gender presentation may have contributed to this. This happened with two different straight therapists, so I refused to see any more therapists.

The experience of the anonymous respondent highlights the need for LGBTQ-specific therapy programs. Such programs do exist and, according to the same survey, a majority of respondents found those programs to be both more welcoming and more helpful than ones with a more general focus. Regardless of the type of agency, survey participants said they benefited most from working with staff who are knowledgeable, nonjudgmental, empathetic, and good listeners.

Carrie Lippy and Emily M. Waters, *"I Didn't Think People Would Take Me Seriously": The Help-Seeking Strategies, Experiences, and Preferences of LGBTQ Survivors*. Harrisburg, PA: National LGBTQ Institute on Intimate Partner Violence, 2021, p. 28. http://unified-solutions.org.

rate than males transitioning to females, although both are much higher than the general adolescent population.

More than half of female-to-male adolescents (50.8 percent) reported at least one attempted suicide in their lifetimes—a figure nearly three times higher than that of all adolescent females. Among male-to-female adolescents, 29.9 percent reported attempting suicide in their lifetimes—a rate three times higher than that of all adolescent males. "The lack of visibility and acceptance in society contributes to these shocking figures about suicide attempts and self-harm in trans young people," says Margaret Unwin, the chief executive of Pace, a mental health charity for LGBTQ people. "While society's attitudes towards transgender people are changing, it is still not fast enough and the negative impacts on trans people's mental health every day are huge."[45]

Adolescents who have not settled on their gender identity also have higher suicide attempt rates than the general adolescent population. Adolescents who have not identified as exclusively male or female have a suicide attempt rate of 41.8 percent—three times higher than that of the general adolescent population. Those adolescents who identify as questioning their genders have a suicide attempt rate of 27.9 percent, double the attempted suicide rate of the general population.

The University of Arizona researchers believe that the differences in suicide rates should serve as a guide to public health officials. "Suicide prevention efforts can be enhanced by attending to variability within transgender populations," write the researchers, "particularly the heightened risk for female to male and nonbinary transgender adolescents."[46]

Suicide Risks Among LGB Youths

Lesbian, gay, and bisexual young people face many of the same pressures and abuses that transgender youths do, including rejection, ridicule, and abuse. These added stresses cause higher levels of anxiety and depression among LGB youths than among their heterosexual counterparts, leading to higher rates of suicidal behaviors.

According to the CDC's 2019 Youth Risk Behavior Survey, 23.4 percent of LGB youths attempted suicide in the past year, a rate 3.6 times higher than that of heterosexual youths (6.4 percent). The survey found that 16 percent of students who are unsure about their sexual identities attempted suicide in the past year, a rate 2.5 times higher than that of heterosexuals.

Unlike transgender adolescents, lesbian and bisexual female adolescents have about the same rates of suicide attempts as their male counterparts, but both are much higher than the general population. Almost a quarter of these young women (23.6 percent) attempted suicide in the last year, a rate three times higher than female heterosexual students (7.9 percent). Among gay and bisexual male students, 23.8 percent attempted suicide in the last year, a rate almost five times higher than their heterosexual counterparts (5.1 percent).

Students who stated they were not sure about their sexual identity also have higher rates of attempted suicide than the heterosexual population. According to the CDC, 15.2 percent of girls and 16.4 percent of boys who were not sure of their sexual identities reported attempting suicide in the past year.

Within the transgender community, females transitioning to male reported a higher attempted suicide rate than males transitioning to female, although the rate for both is higher than that for the general adolescent population.

The Pressures of Growing Up LGBTQ

As a youth, Adam Swanson experienced abuse from his community and his classmates. "Growing up, a queer life felt too dangerous to even imagine,"[47] he says. "I was bullied every single day. I mean, every day. From the minute I got on the bus to the minute I got off the bus. I would spend my lunches in the library hiding under a staircase reading books. . . . It was way safer to be in solitude by myself than it was to be with the other kids."[48]

Swanson was raised in a small town outside of Chicago, a place that seemed especially hostile to the LGBTQ community. "Outside of the school building, there were the presence of oversized church steeples that extended as far as the horizon of our town's Midwestern cornrows," Swanson remembers. "They said God hates fags. Coming out there, even to myself, was not an option."[49]

Life inside the school was worse. Swanson tried to conceal his sexual identity, but his classmates sensed he was different and targeted him for abuse. "School hallways and classrooms were labyrinths crawling with toxic suburban boyhood," Swanson says. "I tried to get by unnoticed, but again and again, my name was found in bathroom stalls, written alongside variations of words like *gay*, *faggot* . . . But unlike boys' fists, at least I could color over those words with a black marker."[50]

Overwhelmed by the bullying, Swanson tried to take his own life—the first time while still in elementary school, at age nine. He survived, and he eventually embraced his sexual identity when he was in college. "At an out-of-state university in Kentucky, I existed in a place where I was unknown to anyone," he recalls. "There, imagining my life became less frightening, and in my sophomore year, I put words to that deeply repressed part of my life. I came out. I busted out! In one day, and out the next. *Of course, we'll always love you!*, they all said, and the relief of telling my family and new friends felt like the life of a new body."[51]

Knowing what LGBTQ kids and teens are going through, Swanson has dedicated his life to suicide prevention. He is now a senior prevention specialist at the Suicide Prevention Resource Center in Chicago. "Life is painful. It's guaranteed pain," Swanson says. "But . . . if we can help people get through moments of pain there's a lot of value to this life, too."[52]

The situation may be even worse than it seems for LGBTQ youth. Under the current reporting systems in most US counties, there is no established way to report a person's sexual orientation or gender identity data when they die. As a result, the true number of suicides in the LGBTQ community cannot be known.

In the meantime, groups such as the Trevor Project, a suicide prevention and crisis intervention organization for LGBTQ youth, are reaching out to young people who may be thinking of taking their own lives. "You may feel like, 'I am the only gay person in my community,' or 'I'm the only trans person in my town,'" says Amit Paley, the CEO and executive director of the Trevor Project. "Those are feelings that can increase the risk of suicide. Our message is, 'You're not alone. There are many people who will celebrate who you are.'"[53]

CHAPTER FOUR

The Impact of Suicide on Survivors

Suicide is widely considered to be a private matter. It often takes place in secret, when the person is alone. Even the phrase *took his or her own life* suggests that suicide is a solitary act. But nothing could be further from the truth. Each suicide affects many people who are left to cope with its powerful aftereffects. "Suicide is a serious public health problem that causes immeasurable pain, suffering, and loss to individuals, families, and communities nationwide,"[54] states the Substance Abuse and Mental Health Services Administration, an agency within the federal government.

Survivor Anguish

Each suicide sends out shockwaves of pain that rock the lives of family, friends, and the community. The death of any loved one causes pain and suffering, but suicide survivors—family members and others who have a close connection to the victim—experience much more than sadness and grief. Because suicide is preventable, survivors often are wracked by feelings of failure and guilt. "Survivors of suicide seem to struggle more with questions of meaning around the death," writes a team of Swedish researchers who studied the effects of suicide on the community. "Survivors often show higher levels of guilt, blame and responsibility for the death"[55] than do people who are mourning deaths that occurred under different circumstances.

María Inés Zamudio struggled with doubts and guilt after the suicide of her sister Alma in 2017. Whenever family members asked about Alma's death, Zamudio felt she was being attacked. "There's a special kind of abuse directed at the families of those who die by suicide," Zamudio observes. "I lost count of the number of people who looked through my pain and asked the questions." One family member commented, "Didn't she live with you?" Another asked where Zamudio was when Alma ended her life. "The questions cut deep," Zamudio recalls.

> They sounded like accusations—even indictments—and played on a loop with different voices for weeks. After my sister's suicide, the guilt grew into a permanent lump in my throat, making it impossible for me to swallow anything other than water. The guilt stole my voice, too. I often responded with my rehearsed statement: My younger sister Alma died following a long battle with a chronic illness.[56]

"There's a special kind of abuse directed at the families of those who die by suicide. I lost count of the number of people who looked through my pain and asked [uncomfortable] questions."[56]

—María Inés Zamudio, suicide survivor

Zamudio, whose family migrated to the United States from Mexico, believes her relatives' discomfort with suicide is partly cultural. "Suicide is not something Mexican families talk about," she says. A common attitude among immigrants, Zamudio says, is "we didn't come all the way here to just give up." The success of making a new life in the United States made some members of Zamudio's family

Each suicide leaves behind family members and friends who must then cope with its powerful aftereffects.

wonder what could be so bad that a person would take her own life. "'What do you have to be sad about?' family members would whisper,"[57] Zamudio recalls.

But it was not just a matter of being sad. Alma had been diagnosed with bipolar disorder years before she took her life. "When she was diagnosed with bipolar disorder, we talked about it, regularly and openly," Zamudio says. I meticulously discussed the information I'd learned from my research. But it wasn't enough."[58]

Feelings of Guilt

Like many suicide survivors, Zamudio blamed herself for failing to prevent her sister's death. "I directed the pain and anger inward," she says. "I wasn't mad at her for leaving me with this trauma and her secrets; she was sick and I couldn't be mad at a sick person. It was easier to be mad at myself. For not finding the right hospital. The right psychiatrist. The right therapist. The right medication. The right job. I had failed the most important job in my life."[59]

A Mother Remembers Her Daughter

In this excerpt from the *Alliance of Hope Blog*, a mother remembers the daughter she lost to suicide:

> I have felt anger at my child for not reaching out to me. . . . But what I see is a mixed-up young girl, who loved her mother and hated upsetting her. I think she felt she could deal with it on her own and I think the lies she told were, in her mind, to protect me. She absolutely hated being the cause of my upset. And she got it wrong, she was too young to sort it out herself, she didn't have the mental skills, she didn't have to protect me. And I believe she wasn't really serious until she did it. I think in her mind it was something she thought about often but never actually got around to doing anything about it. So why tell Mum? She didn't know that thoughts can escalate to action in just a matter of minutes. She made a terrible mistake and paid for it with her life, she couldn't cure herself, and she certainly didn't end up protecting me. But I forgive her, I forgive her everything. She was my little lamb and she got lost.

Stricken, "I Forgive Her Everything," *Alliance of Hope Blog*, Alliance of Hope for Suicide Loss Survivors, February 15, 2021. https://allianceofhope.org.

Zamudio's feelings of failure consumed her. "The guilt haunted me for years," she says. "As much as I tried to get rid of it with individual therapy, group therapy and medication, I couldn't stop punishing myself. I'd isolate myself, feeling like my sadness was contagious. But I kept going to therapy and reciting my daily mantra: 'I did the best I could. It's not my fault.'"[60]

Finally, the years of therapy and repeating her self-affirmation paid off for Zamudio. "A few months ago, I sat on the floor of my new apartment," she wrote in September 2021. "As I looked up at the lavender walls, I smiled. She loved that color. I had no furniture yet, only my record player and the sound of Lauryn Hill's voice singing, 'Forgive them, Father, for they know not what they do.' I got Alma's message. It's time to forgive myself."[61]

The Effects on Siblings

The anguish of being a suicide survivor is especially acute among brothers and sisters of a person who has taken their own life, according to the Swedish researchers who studied mourners. They found that siblings of a suicide are at greater risk of taking their own lives than are siblings who lost a loved one due to another cause of death. Women who survived the death of a sibling by natural causes or accidents had a suicide risk that was 1.55 times higher than that of people who had not lost a loved one. But the suicide risk more than doubled to 3.19 times higher than the nonbereaved population when the cause of death was a suicide. In men, the suicide risk jumped from 1.28 times higher than the nonbereaved when the cause of death was from natural causes or accidents to 2.44 times higher when the cause of death was suicide.

The differences in suicide risks between male and female survivors are mainly social, according to the researchers. "This

With the right kinds of help, those left behind by suicide can recover from feelings of failure and guilt. Many people who seek therapy are able to begin to enjoy life again.

finding might reflect the fact that women place more emphasis on social relationships than men do, particularly when it comes to parents and the family," write the Swedish researchers. "The loss of a sibling could hence have stronger emotional consequences for women which, in turn, could account for a higher risk of suicide."[62]

A young woman writing on the Sibling Survivors Suicide Loss website lost her brother to suicide in 2019, and she remained in deep pain two years later. In a letter addressed to her brother, she describes how devastating the loss has been. "There is not a day that goes by where you are not on my mind in one way or another," she writes. She continues:

I wish I could say that your death has somehow made me a better or stronger person but that's just not the case. I am still broken, I am still coping, still trying to find new meaning in life after whatever my previous life was got shattered to bits.

How is it possible to live your entire life with someone and then in an instant have them ripped from you entirely? You were always someone I looked up to growing up and even into my adult years. You were the smarter, funnier, weirder older brother and I wish I could look you in the eyes now and tell you just how much you mean to me. . . .

I'm doing my best but some days it just really weighs down on me.

You were supposed to be there through all the milestones in my life. You were supposed to be there cracking jokes and playing guitar through all the hard times. You were supposed to be there.

I'm still here and I'm still fighting but sometimes I wish that I would wake up from this bad dream and see you and hug you and tell you just how much I've missed you.[63]

A Sister Grieves for Her Brother

An anonymous poster left a letter for her brother on the Sibling Survivors of Suicide Loss website:

> Dear Brother, 7 weeks ago today you finally succeeded in doing what you have been trying to do since March. I can't bear that, that was the only option left open to you. . . . The trail of heartache you have left behind is devastating. I know you would never want any of us suffering like this. I am so angry at the lack of care you got. . . . Your life mattered. Your life was so very precious. I will have the last image of you etched in my mind forever waving to me as the door opened for you to enter the unit. . . . Did I hug you before you exited the car? I can't remember. Your voice comes to me during the day "Hellooooo, any news." I will never get to hear that again. I so badly want to hear that again. . . . I promise to never forget you. I will treasure your memory deep in my heart for as long as it keeps beating. RIP dear brother. I will love you forever and always.

Guest Poster, "My Brother," Sibling Survivors of Suicide Loss, September 24, 2021. www .siblingsurvivors.com.

The Impact on a Community

The shockwaves of suicide spread far beyond parents and siblings, causing pain and disruption in many lives. The CDC reports that each suicide leaves behind six to thirty-two close friends and family members who are classified as suicide survivors. That means between 285,000 and 1.5 million Americans were suicide survivors in 2020 alone.

But the pain and loss of suicide is not confined to a circle of close friends and family. The CDC has found that an average of 425 people are classmates, coworkers, or other acquaintances of each person who commits suicide. About half of all American adults have known at least one suicide, according to a study by researchers at the University of Kentucky.

Knowing individuals who took their own lives can have a profound effect on a survivor's mental health. Many suicide survivors experience not only pain and grief but also diagnosable conditions, such as depression, anxiety, and post-traumatic stress disorder (PTSD). The researchers at the University of Kentucky found that people who are exposed to suicide are about twice as likely to have diagnosable anxiety as individuals not exposed to suicide. They are also twice as likely to have diagnosable depression and suicidal thoughts. The risks are even greater for close friends and family members. They are four times as likely to suffer PTSD than those who have not been exposed to suicide.

The Economic Costs of Suicide

The costs of suicide are usually measured in the number of lives lost and the pain and suffering of the suicide survivors. But suicide has a social and economic cost as well. Teens and young adults who take their own lives deprive the world of a lifetime of contributions they would make to science, technology, the arts, business, and other human endeavors. Between 2000 and 2019, some 80,165 US children and young adults, aged ten to twenty-four, took their own lives. One can only wonder how many potential Albert Einsteins, Duke Ellingtons, Toni Morrisons, and Steve Jobses never lived to see their twenty-fifth birthdays and never made their world-changing contributions to society.

Although the loss of human genius is incalculable, economists have tried to estimate the financial impact of suicide on a society. They often break the costs of suicides and suicide attempts into two categories: direct and indirect. Direct costs are related to the medical treatment of the people who have harmed themselves in a suicide attempt. These costs typically begin with emergency responses to the suicide attempt, including police, fire department, and ambulance expenses. They can also include the cost of medical care in emergency departments and, if the patient survives the attempt, inpatient hospitalization and follow-up care. In

Survivors may need outpatient or even inpatient treatment for depression and other mental health conditions. Individualized therapy is an important part of treatment.

the case of death, the costs include investigations into the cause of death by medical examiners or coroners.

As high as direct costs are, they typically make up only 3 percent of the overall cost of suicide. The other 97 percent is made up of indirect costs. These involve losses in the person's productivity in the workplace as well as at home due to self-inflicted injury or premature death. Such expenses are computed on the basis of lost wages, lost fringe benefits, and lost contributions at home, including child care, for the time the person is recovering from injuries or, in the case of death, for the expected number of years remaining in the person's productive work life.

In a 2020 study, Australian researchers Christopher M. Doran and Irina Kinchin estimated the costs of youth suicide in the ten countries with the highest human development index, a statistical index created by the United Nations that measures life expectancy, education, and per capita income. Doran and Kinchin calculated the total earnings lost due to a single youth's suicide in the United States to be $835,288. That would suggest that the 80,165 youth suicides since 2000 resulted in about $67 billion in lost earnings.

Researchers at the Heller School for Social Policy and Management at Brandeis University looked at the cost of suicide another way. They estimated that each suicide results in $1.3 million in lost productivity over the course of the person's expected life span. That would put the total loss of productivity from the 80,165 youth suicides since 2000 at more than $104.2 billion.

Calculating the cost of suicide has a practical purpose. It gives health care experts a way of estimating the financial value of money spent on suicide prevention. Based on their calculations, the Brandeis researchers estimate that every $1.00 spent on suicide prevention would save $2.50 in the cost of suicides.

The savings may be even greater than that. The researchers based their analysis only on the direct and indirect costs of the individuals involved in the suicide or suicide attempt. However, research has shown that others are also greatly affected by the suicide. Suicide survivors sometimes are so traumatized that they also stop working for a time while they recover from the loss of the loved one. The survivors also may need outpatient or even inpatient treatment for depression and other mental health conditions stemming from the suicide. In some cases, the survivors even attempt to take their own lives, and the entire cycle starts again. All of these add to the financial costs of the suicide and increase the value of suicide prevention.

CHAPTER FIVE

A Preventable Loss of Life

A premature death is any death that occurs before a person reaches the age of seventy-five. According to the CDC, half of all premature deaths are preventable; that is, they could be avoided by changes in behavior or lifestyle, such as stopping smoking, losing weight, managing blood sugar levels, or not consuming large amounts of alcohol. Deaths by suicide are considered preventable because each one could be avoided by proper medical intervention.

Prevention is complicated by the vast array of risk factors that contribute to a person's decision to commit suicide. As a result, there is no single strategy, no single message, no single treatment or therapy that can prevent all suicides. Public health officials and suicide experts have launched a variety of programs to identify suicidal individuals and intervene in their lives while there is still time to prevent a tragedy. "Like most public health problems, suicide is preventable," states the CDC. It recommends a multipronged approach to reducing the number of suicides and suicide attempts. "Suicide prevention is best achieved by a focus across the individual, relationship, family, community, and societal-levels and across all sectors, private and public."[64]

Starting the Conversation

Most people who are thinking about suicide make some kind of reference to taking their lives. It often is not a straightforward statement. It may be presented as a joke or a commentary on a situation that does not involve the person directly. Nevertheless, references to suicide or "wanting to die" must be taken seriously by friends, family members, teachers, or anyone in the person's life. Many people who attempt suicide do so without ever speaking to a counselor or therapist about their suicidal thoughts. It is up to those around them to pick up on any hints they might provide about their state of mind and not be afraid to help them speak to a professional.

Suicide is not a pleasant topic, and many people try their best to avoid the subject. Often, they are afraid that if they bring up the subject, they will put the thought of suicide into a person's mind, in effect offering suicide as a solution to a problem. Experts say this idea is false. "Talking about suicide does not cause someone to become suicidal," states the Nevada Division of Public and Behavioral Health. "Encouraging someone to talk about pent-up emotions through a frank discussion shows that you care and are willing to help."[65]

Many people, especially parents, worry about discussing suicide with children out of the same fear of introducing them to an idea they would never have on their own. Again, experts say the fear is unfounded. "It sounds weird to say we want to talk about suicide all the time," says John Ackerman, the suicide prevention coordinator at the Center for Suicide Prevention and Research at Nationwide Children's Hospital. "But that is healthy, (and) absolutely a child is less at risk if they don't feel like it's a shut door."[66]

Some people are afraid that asking others about their feelings about sui-

> "Talking about suicide does not cause someone to become suicidal. Encouraging someone to talk about pent-up emotions through a frank discussion shows that you care and are willing to help."[65]
>
> —Nevada Division of Public and Behavioral Health

Many parents hesitate to discuss suicide with teenage children out of fear that they will introduce them to suicidal thoughts.

cide will seem like a criticism because it implies that they have a problem. Christine Yu Moutier suggests that friends and family members can avoid such negative feelings by reassuring the person who is facing problems that "these are human experiences, nothing to feel ashamed of, but they are things we want to know about so we can work on them together."[67]

Watching for Signs

Although talking to suicidal people is the best way to discover their need for help, it is not always enough. Some people take their lives without telling anyone or even dropping hints that they are thinking about it, making discussion impossible. Often, these are the people who are most committed to acting on their suicidal thoughts and plans. "The paradox is that the people who are most intent on committing suicide know that they have to keep their plans to themselves if they are to carry out the act," says Michael Miller, an assistant professor of psychiatry at Harvard Medical School. "Thus, the people most in need of help may be the toughest to save."[68]

Discussing Suicide with Young People

In *Almost Thirteen*, a documentary about the suicide of twelve-year-old Hayden Hunstable, Melinda Moore, a clinical suicidologist and an associate professor of psychology at Eastern Kentucky University, shares her views about discussing suicide with young people:

> Young people tend to not have the kind of resources that adults do, whether it's internal or external. They don't have the life experience to know they'll make it through a break-up or having disappointed somebody. . . . We have to have those difficult conversations, and do it in a safe way, not talking about explicit means, but talking about just the idea of suicide. "If things got so bad that you'd want to kill yourself, or you'd think about harming yourself, what could we do in that moment?" Letting them know that no matter what happens you would never want them to harm themselves, and that it will be okay. "We will figure it out. But in that moment, what can you do? Come get mom or dad, reach out to a trusted adult. Do something to distract, to delay, to soothe yourself in that moment, until you can get somebody to come in and help you with that situation."

Quoted in Hayden's Corner, "Almost Thirteen PSA," YouTube, December 21, 2020. https://youtu.be/JeoHM2_ntfw.

Although people might not say that they are considering suicide, they often show physical and emotional signs of being suicidal. For example, their sleep patterns might change. They might have a hard time getting to sleep, or they might start sleeping excessively. Changes in appetite can also signal the onset of anxiety, depression, or feelings of hopelessness or worthlessness. A lack of energy or a sudden disinterest in things that a person used to care about can also be signs of emotional turmoil. These changes in behavior should not be dismissed as teenage moodiness. Asking about them can be a way to open a dialogue about how the person is feeling.

Screening for Suicidality

Relying on personal observations and conversations is the only way most friends, family members, teachers, and school counselors have of identifying suicidal thinking. As a result, most referrals for suicide counseling are made on a personal, or subjective, basis. Some suicide experts have tried to develop more objective methods for identifying those at risk of taking their lives. For example, researchers at Columbia University developed a questionnaire and method for analyzing the responses to objectively determine whether someone is at risk of suicide and how great the risk might be. The tool, known as the Columbia–Suicide Severity Rating Scale (C-SSRS), or the Columbia Protocol, has been the subject of six hundred scientific studies to determine its effectiveness.

A study published in 2021 in the medical journal *Psychological Medicine* examined eighteen thousand psychiatric emergency department patients in Sweden who were given the six-question C-SSRS questionnaire. The study found that the C-SSRS screener accurately predicted which patients were most at risk of death by suicide over one-week, one-month, and one-year periods. In another study, Atrium Health, a hospital network with forty-two hospitals and more than thirty urgent care centers in Alabama, Georgia, and North Carolina, began implementing the C-SSRS in 2019. By 2021, the health care network saw a 50 percent reduction in suicide deaths.

The results of the C-SSRS test helps health care professionals assess the severity and immediacy of suicide risk, and it suggests how much support the person needs. "Its about saving lives and directing limited resources to the people who actually need them,"[69] says Kelly Posner Gerstenhaber, a clinical professor in the Division of Child and Adolescent Psychiatry at Columbia University and one of the developers of the C-SSRS.

One of the best things about the C-SSRS is that it asks the questions and provides the analysis in simple language. As a result, it can be effectively administered by people who are not medical professionals. In 2014, the US Department of Defense (DOD) began using the C-SSRS as a suicide risk assessment tool. The DOD calls the Columbia Protocol "nothing short of a miracle," adding that the protocol "will help propel us closer to a world without suicide."[70]

A Role for Medical Doctors

Medical doctors are in a unique position to help prevent suicide. Studies show that 75 percent of individuals who later take their lives had visited a doctor within the year before their suicide. Between a half and two-thirds of these visits took place within a month of the suicide. In addition, the suicide rate for patients who were admitted to hospitals with suicidal thoughts and later discharged was thirty-five times higher than the overall US national suicide rate.

Although medical doctors are ideally situated to intervene before suicides occur, they traditionally have not been highly trained in recognizing the signs of impending suicide. As a result, in 2018 the American Medical Association (AMA), the largest association of physicians and medical students in the United States, adopted

Medical doctors are in a unique position to help prevent suicides, yet they have traditionally not been trained to recognize the signs of impending suicide.

Debunking Suicide Myths

To help prevent suicides, individuals should know the facts about the issue. In this excerpt, Kristen Fuller, a family medicine physician, debunks common myths about suicide:

> Myth: Suicide only affects individuals with a mental health condition.
> Fact: Not all people who attempt or die by suicide have mental illness. Relationship problems and other life stressors . . . are also associated with suicidal thoughts and attempts.
>
> Myth: Once an individual is suicidal, he or she will always remain suicidal.
> Fact: Active suicidal ideation is often short-term and situation-specific. . . . An individual with suicidal thoughts and attempts can live a long, successful life.
>
> Myth: Most suicides happen suddenly without warning.
> Fact: Warning signs—verbally or behaviorally—precede most suicides.
>
> Myth: People who die by suicide are selfish and take the easy way out.
> Fact: Typically, people do not die by suicide because they do not want to live—people die by suicide because they want to end their suffering.
>
> Myth: Talking about suicide will lead to and encourage suicide.
> Fact: Talking about suicide not only reduces the stigma, but also allows individuals to seek help, rethink their opinions and share their story with others. We all need to talk more about suicide.

Kristen Fuller, "5 Common Myths About Suicide Debunked," *NAMI Blog,* National Alliance for Mental Illness, September 30, 2020. www.nami.org.

a policy calling for training to help physicians assess suicide risk and counsel at-risk individuals.

In the wake of CDC reports about the 31 percent increase in mental health–related emergency department visits for twelve- to seventeen-year-olds during 2020 as compared to 2019, the AMA adopted a new policy in June 2021 that aims to prevent suicide in young people. The policy calls for the dissemination of educational resources and tools for physicians that address effective suicide prevention. "As a nation we must do everything we can to prioritize children's mental, emotional and behavioral health and step up our efforts to prevent suicide and mitigate suicide risk among our nation's youth," says AMA board member Willie Underwood. "Physicians play a vital role and we must ensure that all physicians who see youth patients, not solely pediatric psychiatrists and addiction medicine physicians, have the ability, capacity, and access to the tools needed to identify when a young person is experiencing a period of imminent risk and help prevent suicide attempts."[71]

Suicide Prevention Apps

As part of its focus on youth suicide, the AMA also declared its support for the development of novel technologies and therapeutics. Because a high percentage of young people use mobile phones, mental health organizations and private companies have developed several suicide prevention apps. One of these is the Virtual Hope Box. It grew out of the clinical practice of having suicidal patients place photos and other objects into a box to help them find and remember their reasons for living. The Virtual Hope Box works the same way, with users uploading images, lists of things they want to do, and future goals to the app. When users feel suicidal, they can check their Virtual Hope Box to distract themselves from their suicidal thoughts and remind themselves of all the reasons they have to live.

Another app, notOK, takes a more direct approach to suicide prevention. Developed by a teen who struggled with suicidal thoughts, the app features a large, red "panic" button that enables users to alert a support group that they need help. When a

BetterHelp is a medical care app that connects the person using it to licensed mental health professionals.

user pushes the button, the app sends the user's GPS location to five trusted contacts along with the following message: "Hey, I'm not OK! Please call, text, or come find me."[72]

An app called BetterHelp is similar, but it connects the user to licensed mental health professionals rather than a support group. Available as a paid subscription, BetterHelp provides users with unlimited access to licensed therapists.

One of the most disturbing aspects of suicide is that people who take their lives have made a conscious decision to do so. The decision may be clouded by mental illness, drugs, or alcohol, but it remains a conscious decision. That is why suicide is referred to as intentional self-harm in the CDC's official statistics on causes of death. But the very thing that makes suicide so tragic— its intentionality—is the same thing that gives suicide prevention advocates hope. Because suicide is a decision, not an accident or a disease that springs up out of nowhere, it can be addressed. The decision can be postponed long enough for the person to get help. The decision can change. People who want to end their lives can choose to live, and they can go on to have long, productive, and happy lives.

Introduction: A Troubling Trend

1. Quoted in Hayden's Corner, "Almost Thirteen PSA," YouTube, December 21, 2020. https://youtu.be/JeoHM2_ntfw.
2. Quoted in Hayden's Corner, "Brad Hunstable on the Tragic Death of His Son Hayden," YouTube, May 1, 2020. https://youtu.be/VJTHFhVyyql.
3. Quoted in Gustaf Kilander, "Dad Says Covid Lockdown Was Behind 12-Year-Old Son's Suicide," *The Independent* (London), February 17, 2021. www.independent.co.uk.
4. Vivek H. Murthy, "Protecting Youth Mental Health: The U.S. Surgeon General's Advisory," US Public Health Service, 2021. https://www.hhs.gov.
5. Quoted in Hayden's Corner, "Almost Thirteen PSA."

Chapter One: Social Media as a Risk Factor for Teen Girls

6. Quoted in Kate Linebaugh, "The Facebook Files, Part 2: 'We Make Body Image Issues Worse,'" *The Journal* (podcast), *Wall Street Journal,* September 14, 2021. www.wsj.com.
7. Quoted in Linebaugh, "The Facebook Files, Part 2."
8. Quoted in Linebaugh, "The Facebook Files, Part 2."
9. Quoted in Linebaugh, "The Facebook Files, Part 2."
10. Quoted in Georgia Wells, Jeff Horwitz, and Deepa Seetharaman, "Facebook Knows Instagram Is Toxic for Teen Girls, Company Documents Show," *Wall Street Journal,* September 14, 2021. www.wsj.com.
11. Quoted in Wells, Horwitz, and Seetharaman, "Facebook Knows Instagram Is Toxic for Teen Girls, Company Documents Show."
12. Quoted in Wells, Horwitz, and Seetharaman, "Facebook Knows Instagram Is Toxic for Teen Girls, Company Documents Show."
13. Quoted in Wells, Horwitz, and Seetharaman, "Facebook Knows Instagram Is Toxic for Teen Girls, Company Documents Show."
14. Quoted in Wells, Horwitz, and Seetharaman, "Facebook Knows Instagram Is Toxic for Teen Girls, Company Documents Show."
15. Quoted in Linebaugh, "The Facebook Files, Part 2."
16. Quoted in Erin Woo, "Teenage Girls Say Instagram's Mental Health Impacts Are No Surprise," *New York Times,* October 5, 2021. www.nytimes.com.

17. Quoted in Wells, Horwitz, and Seetharaman, "Facebook Knows Instagram Is Toxic for Teen Girls, Company Documents Show."
18. Quoted in Wells, Horwitz, and Seetharaman, "Facebook Knows Instagram Is Toxic for Teen Girls, Company Documents Show."
19. Quoted in Fox News, *Tucker Carlson Tonight*, season 6, episode 194, September 29, 2021.
20. Quoted in Shirin Ghaffary, "It's Getting Harder for People to Believe That Facebook Is a Net Good for Society," Vox, September 16, 2021. www.vox.com.
21. Quoted in *Rev* (blog), "Facebook Head of Safety Testimony on Mental Health Effects: Full Senate Hearing Transcript," September 30, 2021. www.rev.com.
22. Quoted in *Rev* (blog), "Facebook Head of Safety Testimony on Mental Health Effects: Full Senate Hearing Transcript."
23. Quoted in Linebaugh, "The Facebook Files, Part 2."
24. Quoted in Linebaugh, "The Facebook Files, Part 2."

Chapter Two: The Impact of the Pandemic on Teen Mental Health

25. Quoted in Christine Kim, "Orange County Family Shares Teen Suicide Story as Pandemic Warning to Other Parents," NBC4 Los Angeles, January 19, 2021. www.nbclosangeles.com.
26. Quoted in Kim, "Orange County Family Shares Teen Suicide Story as Pandemic Warning to Other Parents."
27. Quoted in Children's Hospital Colorado, "Children's Hospital Colorado Declares a 'State of Emergency' for Youth Mental Health," May 25, 2021. www.childrenscolorado.org.
28. Quoted in Morgan Haefner, "'Overrun with Kids Attempting Suicide': Children's Colorado Declares State of Emergency," Becker's Hospital Review, May 26, 2021. www.beckershospitalreview.com.
29. Ellen Yard et al., "Emergency Department Visits for Suspected Suicide Attempts Among Persons Aged 12–25 Years Before and During the COVID-19 Pandemic—United States, January 2019–May 2021," CDC, June 18, 2021. https://www.cdc.gov/mmwr/volumes/70/wr/mm7024e1.htm?s_cid=mm7024e1_w.
30. Quoted in Allyson Chiu, "CDC: ER Visits for Suspected Suicide Attempts Among Teenage Girls Rose During Pandemic," *Washington Post,* June 11, 2021. www.washingtonpost.com.
31. Quoted in Rhitu Chatterjee, "Child Psychiatrists Warn That the Pandemic May Be Driving Up Kids' Suicide Risk," NPR, February 2, 2021. www.npr.org.
32. Quoted in Maura Hohman, "Girls Are Attempting Suicide More During the Pandemic. Here's How Parents Can Help," *Today*, September 29, 2021. www.today.com.
33. Quoted in Chatterjee, "Child Psychiatrists Warn That the Pandemic May Be Driving Up Kids' Suicide Risk."

34. Quoted in Chatterjee, "Child Psychiatrists Warn That the Pandemic May Be Driving Up Kids' Suicide Risk."
35. Quoted in Jayne O'Donnell and Anne Saker, "Teen Suicide Is Soaring. Do Spotty Mental Health and Addiction Treatment Share Blame?," *USA Today,* March 19, 2018. www.usatoday.com.
36. Quoted in Chatterjee, "Child Psychiatrists Warn That the Pandemic May Be Driving Up Kids' Suicide Risk."
37. Quoted in Chatterjee, "Child Psychiatrists Warn That the Pandemic May Be Driving Up Kids' Suicide Risk."
38. Quoted in Chatterjee, "Child Psychiatrists Warn That the Pandemic May Be Driving Up Kids' Suicide Risk."
39. Quoted in Chatterjee, "Child Psychiatrists Warn That the Pandemic May Be Driving Up Kids' Suicide Risk."
40. Quoted in Chatterjee, "Child Psychiatrists Warn That the Pandemic May Be Driving Up Kids' Suicide Risk."

Chapter Three: LGBTQ Teens at Risk

41. Quoted in Patrick Strudwick, "Nearly Half of Young Transgender People Have Attempted Suicide—UK survey," *The Guardian*, November 19, 2014. www.theguardian.com.
42. Quoted in Alia E. Dastagir, "Young, Transgender and Fighting a Years-Long Battle Against Suicidal Thoughts," *USA Today,* November 28, 2018. www.usatoday.com.
43. Quoted in Dastagir, "Young, Transgender and Fighting a Years-Long Battle Against Suicidal Thoughts."
44. Quoted in Dastagir, "Young, Transgender and Fighting a Years-Long Battle Against Suicidal Thoughts."
45. Quoted in Strudwick, "Nearly Half of Young Transgender People Have Attempted Suicide."
46. Russell B. Toomey et al., "Transgender Adolescent Suicide Behavior," *Pediatrics*, October 2018. https://pediatrics.aappublications.org.
47. Adam Swanson, "The Night I Came Out to Police Officers in an Emergency Room in Chicago," Oprah Daily, September 14, 2020. www.oprahdaily.com.
48. Quoted in Dastagir, "Young, Transgender and Fighting a Years-Long Battle Against Suicidal Thoughts."
49. Swanson, "The Night I Came Out to Police Officers in an Emergency Room in Chicago."
50. Swanson, "The Night I Came Out to Police Officers in an Emergency Room in Chicago."
51. Swanson, "The Night I Came Out to Police Officers in an Emergency Room in Chicago."
52. Swanson, "The Night I Came Out to Police Officers in an Emergency Room in Chicago."

53. Quoted in Dastagir, "Young, Transgender and Fighting a Years-Long Battle Against Suicidal Thoughts."

Chapter Four: The Impact of Suicide on Survivors

54. Substance Abuse and Mental Health Services Administration, "Suicide Prevention," October 14, 2021. www.samhsa.gov.
55. Mikael Rostila et al., "Suicide Following the Death of a Sibling: A Nationwide Follow-Up Study from Sweden," *BMJ Open,* April 26, 2013. https://bmjopen.bmj.com.
56. María Inés Zamudio, "Suicide Isn't Something Mexican Families Talk About. Years After My Sister's Death, I Finally Stopped Blaming Myself," *The Lily,* September 17, 2021. www.thelily.com.
57. Zamudio, "Suicide Isn't Something Mexican Families Talk About."
58. Zamudio, "Suicide Isn't Something Mexican Families Talk About."
59. Zamudio, "Suicide Isn't Something Mexican Families Talk About."
60. Zamudio, "Suicide Isn't Something Mexican Families Talk About."
61. Zamudio, "Suicide Isn't Something Mexican Families Talk About."
62. Rostila et al., "Suicide Following the Death of a Sibling."
63. Anonymous, "For My Older Brother," Sibling Survivors Suicide Loss, February 24, 2021. www.siblingsurvivors.com.

Chapter Five: A Preventable Loss of Life

64. Deb Stone et al., *Preventing Suicide: A Technical Package of Policy, Programs, and Practices.* Atlanta: National Center for Injury Prevention and Control, Centers for Disease Control and Prevention, 2017, p. 7.
65. Office of Suicide Prevention, "Truth or Myth: About Adult Suicide," Nevada Division of Public and Behavioral Health, 2021. https://suicideprevention.nv.gov.
66. Quoted in Laura Ziegler, "With Teen Suicide on the Rise in Kansas City, Adults Ask Young People What They Need," KCUR 89.3, December 20, 2018. www.kcur.org.
67. Quoted in Hohman, "Girls Are Attempting Suicide More During the Pandemic."
68. Quoted in Patrick J. Skerrett, "Suicide Often Not Preceded by Warnings," *Harvard Health Blog*, Harvard Medical School, October 29, 2015. www.health.harvard.edu.
69. Quoted in Yahoo! News, "Groundbreaking Study Proves Columbia Protocol Predicts Those at Risk for Imminent Suicide," July 19, 2021. www.yahoo.com.
70. Quoted in Yahoo! News, "Groundbreaking Study Proves Columbia Protocol Predicts Those at Risk for Imminent Suicide."
71. Quoted in American Medical Association, "AMA Adopts Policy to Address Increases in Youth Suicide and Save Lives," June 16, 2021. www.ama-assn.org.
72. Quoted in "Top Rated Apps for Suicide Prevention," Suicide Prevention Alliance, 2021. https://www.suicidepreventionalliance.org.

Alliance of Hope for Suicide Loss Survivors

www.allianceofhope.org

The Alliance of Hope for Suicide Loss Survivors is a non-profit organization that provides information to help survivors understand the complex emotional aftermath of suicide. Its website features a blog, bookstore, and memorials.

American Association of Suicidology (AAS)

www.suicidology.org

The AAS promotes research, public awareness programs, public education, and training for professionals and volunteers. In addition, the AAS serves as a national clearinghouse for information on suicide. Its mission is to promote the understanding and prevention of suicide and support those who have been affected by it.

American Foundation for Suicide Prevention (AFSP)

www.afsp.org

Established in 1987, the AFSP is a voluntary health organization. The foundation is dedicated to saving lives and bringing hope to those affected by suicide. It offers those affected by suicide a nationwide community and supports them through education, advocacy, and research.

Jason Foundation

www.jasonfoundation.com

The Jason Foundation provides curriculum material to schools, parents, and teens about how teen suicide can be prevented. It is dedicated to the prevention of the silent epidemic of youth suicide through educational and awareness programs that equip young people, educators, youth workers, and parents with the tools and resources to help identify and assist at-risk youth.

National Suicide Prevention Lifeline

https://suicidepreventionlifeline.org

(800) 273-8255

The National Suicide Prevention Lifeline is a national network of local crisis centers. It operates twenty-four hours a day, seven days a week, and provides free and confidential support for people experiencing a suicidal crisis or emotional distress.

Sibling Survivors of Suicide Loss

www.siblingsurvivors.com

The Sibling Survivors of Suicide Loss site aims to provide a safe place for anyone who has lost a sister or brother to suicide. It is a place for people who have lost a sibling to suicide to share memories and photos and discuss their feelings and experiences. It is also a place to connect with others who have lost a sister or brother to suicide.

Trevor Project

www.thetrevorproject.org

Founded in 1998 by the creators of the Academy Award–winning short film *Trevor*, the Trevor Project is a national organization providing crisis intervention and suicide prevention services to LGBTQ young people ages thirteen to twenty-four.

Books

Amy Bleuel, *Project Semicolon: Your Story Isn't Over*. New York: HarperCollins, 2017.

Mary Quirk, *Teen Suicide*. San Diego: ReferencePoint, 2021.

Bonnie Szumski, *Overcoming Suicidal Thoughts*. San Diego: ReferencePoint, 2022.

Cynthia Waldt, *Suicide Is Not a Four Letter Word: Straight Talk About Suicide When It Matters Most*. Pennsauken, NJ: BookBaby, 2022.

Angela L. Williams, *Suicide Information for Teens*. Detroit: Omnigraphics, 2020.

Internet Sources

Dana Alkhouri, "Pandemic's Mental Health Burden Heaviest Among Young Adults," ABC News, February 21, 2021. https://abcnews.go.com.

Rhitu Chatterjee, "Child Psychiatrists Warn That the Pandemic May Be Driving Up Kids' Suicide Risk," NPR, February 2, 2021. www.npr.org.

Perri Klass, "How to Help When Adolescents Have Suicidal Thoughts," *New York Times*, February 6, 2021. www.nytimes.com.

Kate Linebaugh, "The Facebook Files, Part 2: 'We Make Body Image Issues Worse,'" *The Journal* (podcast), *Wall Street Journal*, September 14, 2021. www.wsj.com.

Alan Mozes, "As Social Media Time Rises, so Does Teen Girls' Suicide Risk," *U.S. News & World Report,* February 16, 2021. www.usnews.com.

INDEX